ADHD (

KIDS

JANA SHANNON

TABLE OF CONTENT

Disclaimer

The information provided in this cookbook is for educational and informational purposes only. It is not intended to be a substitute for professional medical advice, diagnosis, or treatment.

Always seek the advice of your physician or other qualified health provider with any questions you may have regarding a medical condition.

The recipes and dietary suggestions included are based on general principles and may not be suitable for everyone.

Individual dietary needs and health conditions vary, and it is essential to consult with a healthcare professional before making significant changes to your diet.

The author and publisher disclaim responsibility for any effects resulting directly or indirectly from the use or misuse of the information provided in this cookbook.

Introduction

As a parent, have you ever felt overwhelmed by your child's ADHD symptoms? Do you find yourself wondering if there's a natural way to support their health and well-being?

You're not alone in this journey, and the answer might be closer than you think – right on your dinner plate.

Imagine a world where your child's focus sharpens, their energy stabilizes, and their mood brightens – all through the power of nutrition.

This isn't just a dream; it's a possibility that lies within reach. But here's the question that might be on your mind: How can you navigate the complex world of nutrition while juggling the unique needs of a child with ADHD?

That's exactly why this book exists. It's not just another cookbook; it's your compass in the sometimes confusing landscape of ADHD nutrition.

By the time you turn the last page, you'll have a treasure trove of knowledge at your fingertips.

You'll understand which foods can fuel your child's brain and body, and which ones might be holding them back.

You'll have a pantry full of ADHD-friendly ingredients and a repertoire of delicious, kid-approved recipes that make healthy eating a joy, not a chore.

But what sets this book apart? It's not just about what to eat – it's about how to make it work in real life.

I'm talking about practical shopping lists, time-saving tips, and a 30-day meal plan that takes the guesswork out of "What's for dinner?"

It's as if you have a nutrition expert and a chef present in your kitchen, providing you with guidance at every step.

Perhaps you're thinking, "Does modifying our diet truly have an impact?" The answer is a resounding yes.

While diet isn't a magic cure-all, countless families have seen remarkable improvements in their children's ADHD symptoms through thoughtful nutrition.

And the best part? These changes don't just benefit your child with ADHD – they can boost the health and well-being of your entire family.

Remember, you're not alone on this journey. Every recipe, every tip, and every bit of advice in this book comes from a place of understanding and support.

We're in this together, and with each meal you prepare, you're taking a powerful step towards a brighter, more balanced future for your child.

So, are you ready to embark on this flavorful adventure? Turn the page, and let's dive into the principles of the ADHD diet. Your transformative journey starts now – and it's going to be delicious!

CHAPTER 1

Principles of the ADHD Diet

1. **Prioritize Protein:** Protein-rich foods are essential for stabilizing blood sugar levels and fueling your child's brain.

   Incorporating lean meats, fish, eggs, beans, and nuts into meals helps improve focus and concentration. Start the day with a protein-packed breakfast to set a solid foundation.

2. **Choose Complex Carbohydrates:** Opt for whole grains, vegetables, and legumes over refined carbs.

   Complex carbs release energy slowly, which helps maintain steady blood sugar levels, reducing mood swings and hyperactivity.

   A balanced plate with fiber-rich carbs promotes lasting energy and better attention.

3. **Focus on Omega-3 Fats:** Omega-3 fatty acids are known to support brain function and reduce ADHD symptoms. Foods like salmon, flaxseeds, walnuts, and chia seeds are packed with these healthy fats.

Make it a habit to include omega-3s in your child's meals for improved cognitive health.

4. **Limit Sugar and Artificial Additives:** High sugar and processed foods can trigger hyperactivity and make it harder for your child to focus.

   Steer clear of sugary snacks, sodas, and foods with artificial dyes, preservatives, and flavorings. Instead, offer whole fruits and naturally sweetened options.

5. **Stay Hydrated:** Water is often overlooked but essential for brain function. Ensure your child drinks enough water throughout the day to stay hydrated and maintain concentration.

By following these simple yet effective principles, you can positively impact your child's ADHD symptoms and set them on a path to better health and focus.

Benefits of ADHD Diet

1. **Improved Focus and Attention:** By fueling your child with brain-boosting foods like lean proteins and omega-3 fatty acids, you'll help enhance their ability to concentrate and stay on task.

   The right nutrients can sharpen their focus, making schoolwork and daily activities easier to manage.

2. **Stabilized Energy Levels:** ADHD can cause fluctuations in energy, often resulting in hyperactivity or fatigue.

A diet rich in complex carbohydrates, proteins, and healthy fats stabilizes blood sugar levels, providing steady energy throughout the day. This means fewer energy crashes and more consistent behavior.

3. **Reduced Hyperactivity and Impulsivity:** Eliminating processed foods, sugary snacks, and artificial additives can significantly reduce hyperactive behaviors.

The ADHD diet emphasizes whole, natural foods, which help balance brain chemistry and reduce impulsive actions.

4. **Better Mood Regulation:** The foods you provide can have a direct impact on your child's mood.

Foods rich in essential nutrients, particularly those with high levels of vitamins and minerals like magnesium and zinc, support emotional balance, helping to reduce irritability, anxiety, and mood swings.

5. **Support for Overall Brain Health:** Omega-3 fatty acids, found in fish and flaxseeds, are crucial for brain development and function.

A diet high in these healthy fats nurtures your child's brain, supporting long-term cognitive health and development.

Foods to Eat

Lean Proteins: Include sources like chicken, turkey, fish, eggs, tofu, and legumes. These foods help stabilize blood sugar and provide the necessary amino acids for neurotransmitter production, enhancing focus and mood.

Fatty Fish: Fish such as salmon, mackerel, and sardines are rich in omega-3 fatty acids, which are crucial for brain health.

Aim to include fatty fish in your child's diet at least twice a week to support cognitive function and reduce ADHD symptoms.

Whole Grains: Go for whole grains like quinoa, brown rice, oats, and whole-wheat bread for a healthier choice.

These complex carbohydrates provide a steady release of energy, helping to maintain focus and reduce irritability.

Fruits and Vegetables: A colorful variety of fruits and vegetables is essential for providing vitamins, minerals, and antioxidants.

Berries, leafy greens, carrots, and bananas are particularly beneficial. Aim for at least five servings a day to ensure your child gets a wide range of nutrients.

Nuts and Seeds: Almonds, walnuts, chia seeds, and flaxseeds offer abundant healthy fats and protein. They can be added to smoothies, yogurt, or eaten as snacks, providing essential nutrients that support brain function.

Healthy Fats: Incorporate sources of healthy fats, such as avocado, olive oil, and coconut oil. These fats support brain health and help absorb fat-soluble vitamins, enhancing overall nutrition.

Dairy Alternatives: If your child is sensitive to dairy, consider alternatives like almond milk, coconut yogurt, or oat milk. These options often come fortified with essential vitamins and minerals, making them a suitable choice.

Herbs and Spices: Fresh herbs like basil, cilantro, and parsley not only add flavor but also come packed with antioxidants. Spices such as turmeric and ginger have anti-inflammatory properties that can benefit overall health.

Foods to Avoid

Sugary Foods and Drinks: Sugar can lead to spikes and crashes in blood sugar levels, causing mood swings, hyperactivity, and difficulty concentrating.

Avoid sugary snacks, candies, sodas, and fruit juices with added sugars. Instead, opt for naturally sweetened options like whole fruits.

Artificial Additives: Artificial colors, flavors, and preservatives have been linked to increased hyperactivity in some children with ADHD.

These are often found in processed foods, candy, and packaged snacks. Check labels for ingredients like food dyes (Red 40, Yellow 5) and synthetic flavorings.

Caffeine: Although caffeine can have a calming effect on some individuals, it is generally not recommended for children with ADHD.

Caffeine, found in sodas, energy drinks, and even chocolate, can interfere with sleep and exacerbate impulsivity.

Highly Processed Foods: Processed foods like chips, fast food, and frozen meals are often high in unhealthy fats, sodium, and additives that can worsen ADHD symptoms.

Try to stick with whole, unprocessed foods as much as you can.

Simple Carbohydrates: White bread, sugary cereals, and other refined carbs cause rapid spikes in blood sugar, leading to energy crashes and irritability.

Swap these out for complex carbs like whole grains and vegetables, which provide steady energy.

Full Shopping List

Proteins

- Chicken breast (skinless, lean)
- Turkey breast (skinless, lean)
- Salmon (fresh or canned)
- Tuna (fresh or canned in water)
- Eggs
- Tofu

- Lentils
- Chickpeas
- Black beans
- Kidney beans
- Low-fat cottage cheese
- Plain Greek yogurt
- Almonds, walnuts, cashews
- Nut butters (unsweetened)

Fruits
- Apples
- Bananas
- Berries (blueberries, strawberries, raspberries)
- Oranges
- Pears
- Peaches
- Grapes
- Kiwi
- Avocados
- Cherries
- Melons (cantaloupe, honeydew)
- Pineapple

Vegetables
- Spinach

- Kale
- Broccoli
- Carrots
- Zucchini
- Sweet potatoes
- Bell peppers (red, yellow, green)
- Cauliflower
- Green beans
- Asparagus
- Brussels sprouts
- Cucumbers
- Tomatoes
- Avocados

Whole Grains

- Oats (steel-cut or rolled)
- Brown rice
- Quinoa
- Barley
- Whole-wheat bread
- Whole-grain pasta
- Buckwheat
- Millet

Healthy Fats

- Extra virgin olive oil
- Flaxseeds
- Chia seeds
- Ground flaxseed
- Walnuts
- Sunflower seeds
- Pumpkin seeds

Dairy and Alternatives

- Unsweetened almond milk
- Unsweetened soy milk
- Low-fat milk
- Low-fat cheese (mozzarella, cheddar)
- Greek yogurt (plain, unsweetened)

Herbs and Spices

- Turmeric
- Cinnamon
- Ginger
- Oregano
- Thyme
- Rosemary
- Basil

CHAPTER 2

Breakfast Recipes

Sweet Potato and Black Bean Breakfast Bowl

- **Preparation Time:** 25 minutes
- **Serves:** 2
- **Size per Serving:** 1 bowl (approximately 250g)

Ingredients:

- 1 medium sweet potato, peeled and diced
- 1/2 cup cooked black beans, rinsed
- 1/2 avocado, diced
- 1 tablespoon olive oil
- 1/4 teaspoon ground cumin
- 1/4 teaspoon paprika
- Salt and pepper, to taste
- 1 tablespoon fresh cilantro, chopped
- 1 tablespoon lime juice
- 2 tablespoons pumpkin seeds (optional for added crunch)

Nutritional Information: Calories: 220 | Total Fat: 10g | Saturated Fat: 1.5g | Cholesterol: 0mg | Sodium: 160mg | Total Carbohydrates: 30g | Dietary Fiber: 8g | Sugar: 5g | Protein: 6g

Instructions:

1. Preheat the oven to 400°F (200°C).

2. Toss the diced sweet potatoes in olive oil, cumin, paprika, salt, and pepper. Spread evenly on a baking sheet.

3. Roast the sweet potatoes for 20 minutes or until tender, flipping halfway through.

4. While roasting the sweet potatoes, heat the black beans on medium heat in a pan, adding a pinch of salt if required.

5. Once the sweet potatoes are ready, divide them between two bowls.

6. Add the warmed black beans, diced avocado, and sprinkle with fresh cilantro.

7. Drizzle each bowl with lime juice and sprinkle pumpkin seeds on top if using.

Serving Suggestions:

- Serve warm, with a side of fresh fruit or a green smoothie for a complete meal.
- You can also add a poached egg for extra protein.

Blueberry Oat Pancakes

- **Preparation Time:** 20 minutes
- **Serves:** 4
- **Size per Serving:** 2 pancakes (approximately 150g)

Ingredients:

- 1 cup rolled oats (gluten-free)
- 1/2 cup almond flour
- 1/2 teaspoon baking powder
- 1/4 teaspoon cinnamon
- 1/4 teaspoon salt
- 1/2 cup unsweetened almond milk
- 1 large egg
- 1 tablespoon maple syrup (optional)
- 1 teaspoon vanilla extract
- 1/2 cup fresh or frozen blueberries
- 1 tablespoon coconut oil (for cooking)

Nutritional Information: Calories: 160 | Total Fat: 7g | Saturated Fat: 1g | Cholesterol: 45mg | Sodium: 100mg |

Total Carbohydrates: 20g | Dietary Fiber: 3g | Sugar: 4g | Protein: 5g

Instructions:

1. Pulse the rolled oats in the blender until they are ground into a coarse flour.
2. In a mixing bowl, combine the oat flour, almond flour, baking powder, cinnamon, and salt.
3. In a separate bowl, whisk together the almond milk, egg, maple syrup (if using), and vanilla extract.
4. Add the wet ingredients to the dry ingredients, mixing gently until just combined, then fold in the blueberries.
5. Place a non-stick skillet over medium heat and add a small amount of coconut oil.
6. Pour 1/4 cup of batter onto the skillet for each pancake and cook for 2-3 minutes, until bubbles appear on the surface.
7. Flip and cook for 2-3 minutes longer, until golden brown. Repeat with the remaining batter.

Serving Suggestions:

- Top with extra blueberries and a light drizzle of maple syrup or almond butter.

Smashed Peas and Avocado Toast

- **Preparation Time:** 10 minutes
- **Serves:** 2
- **Size per Serving:** 1 slice (approximately 150g)

Ingredients:

- 1 ripe avocado
- 1/2 cup cooked green peas
- 2 slices whole grain gluten-free bread, toasted
- 1 tablespoon lemon juice
- 1 tablespoon olive oil
- Salt and pepper to taste
- 1 tablespoon fresh mint, chopped (optional)
- 1 tablespoon hemp seeds (optional, for garnish)

Nutritional Information: Calories: 290 | Total Fat: 18g | Saturated Fat: 3g | Cholesterol: 0mg | Sodium: 180mg | Total Carbohydrates: 28g | Dietary Fiber: 9g | Sugar: 2g | Protein: 6g

Instructions:

1. In a small bowl, mash the avocado and cooked peas together until mostly smooth but still a little chunky.
2. Add the lemon juice, olive oil, salt, and pepper, then mix until thoroughly combined.

3. Spread the mashed avocado and pea mixture evenly onto the toasted bread slices.

4. Sprinkle with fresh mint and hemp seeds (if using).

Serving Suggestions:

- Serve immediately with a side of fresh fruit like orange slices or berries.

Turkey and Spinach Egg Muffins

- **Preparation Time:** 20 minutes
- **Serves:** 6 (12 muffins)
- **Size per Serving:** 2 muffins (approximately 200g)

Ingredients:

- 8 large eggs
- 1/2 cup cooked turkey breast, diced
- 1 cup fresh spinach, chopped
- 1/4 cup unsweetened almond milk
- 1/4 teaspoon salt
- 1/4 teaspoon black pepper
- 1 tablespoon olive oil (for lightly greasing the muffin tin)
- 1/2 teaspoon garlic powder (optional)
- 1/4 cup diced bell peppers (optional, for added color)

Nutritional Information: Calories: 130 | Total Fat: 8g | Saturated Fat: 2g | Cholesterol: 190 mg | Sodium: 280mg | Total Carbohydrates: 1g | Dietary Fiber: 0g | Sugar: 0g | Protein: 11g

Instructions:

1. Preheat your oven to 350°F (175°C) and lightly grease a muffin tin with olive oil.

2. In a large mixing bowl, whisk the eggs, almond milk, salt, pepper, and garlic powder (if using).

3. Stir in the diced turkey, chopped spinach, and bell peppers (if using).

4. Carefully pour the egg mixture into the muffin tin cups, filling each one to about three-quarters full.

5. Bake for 18 to 20 minutes, or until the muffins are fully cooked and lightly browned on the top.

6. Allow the muffins to cool slightly before gently taking them out of the tin.

Serving Suggestions:

- Serve while warm, accompanied by fresh fruit or a small salad.

Coconut Yogurt Parfait

- **Preparation Time:** 10 minutes
- **Serves:** 2
- **Size per Serving:** 1 bowl (about 200g)

Ingredients:

- 1 cup unsweetened coconut yogurt
- 1/2 cup mixed berries (blueberries, strawberries, raspberries)
- 2 tablespoons chia seeds
- 2 tablespoons unsweetened shredded coconut
- 1 tablespoon of raw honey or maple syrup (optional for sweetness)
- 2 tablespoons gluten-free granola (optional, for added crunch)

Nutritional Information: Calories: 180 | Total Fat: 9g | Saturated Fat: 7g | Cholesterol: 0mg | Sodium: 15mg | Total Carbohydrates: 22g | Dietary Fiber: 6g | Sugar: 12g | Protein: 3g

Instructions:

1. In two bowls or glasses, layer 1/2 cup of coconut yogurt in each.
2. Top each with 1/4 cup mixed berries.

3. Sprinkle 1 tablespoon of chia seeds and 1 tablespoon of shredded coconut on each.

4. Drizzle with honey or maple syrup if desired.

5. If using, add a tablespoon of gluten-free granola on top for crunch.

Serving Suggestions:

- This parfait pairs well with a handful of nuts or seeds for added protein.

Kale and Mushroom Frittata

- **Preparation Time:** 25 minutes
- **Serves:** 4
- **Size per Serving:** 1 slice (about 150g)

Ingredients:

- 1 tablespoon olive oil
- 1/2 cup chopped kale
- 1/2 cup sliced mushrooms (button or cremini)
- 1/4 cup diced onion
- 6 large eggs
- 1/4 cup unsweetened almond milk
- 1/4 teaspoon salt
- 1/4 teaspoon black pepper
- 1/4 teaspoon garlic powder

Nutritional Information: Calories: 130 | Total Fat: 9g | Saturated Fat: 2g | Cholesterol: 186 mg | Sodium: 220mg | Total Carbohydrates: 3g | Dietary Fiber: 1g | Sugar: 1g | Protein: 10g

Instructions:

1. Preheat your oven to 350°F (175°C).
2. Pour olive oil into a medium oven-safe skillet and heat it on medium.
3. Add the chopped onion and cook until it's soft, which should take about 3-4 minutes.
4. Add the mushrooms and kale, and cook for an additional 3-4 minutes, until the mushrooms are tender and the kale is wilted.
5. In a separate bowl, whisk together the eggs, almond milk, salt, pepper, and garlic powder.
6. Pour the egg mixture into the skillet, stirring gently to distribute the vegetables evenly.
7. Let the frittata cook on the stovetop for 2-3 minutes, until the edges begin to set.
8. Transfer the skillet to the oven and bake for 10-12 minutes, or until the eggs are fully set.

9. After removing it from the oven, let it cool slightly before cutting it into servings.

Serving Suggestions:

- Serve warm with a side of fresh fruit or a small salad for a well-balanced breakfast.

Quinoa and Chia Seed Breakfast Porridge

- **Preparation Time:** 20 minutes
- **Serves:** 4
- **Size per Serving:** 1 bowl (approximately 150g)

Ingredients:

- 1 cup quinoa, rinsed
- 2 cups unsweetened almond milk
- 1 tablespoon chia seeds
- 1 teaspoon cinnamon
- 1 teaspoon vanilla extract
- 1 tablespoon maple syrup (optional)
- 1/4 cup chopped almonds
- 1/4 cup fresh berries (blueberries, strawberries, etc.)
- 1 tablespoon flax seeds (optional, for garnish)

Nutritional Information: Calories: 220 | Total Fat: 7g | Saturated Fat: 0.5g | Cholesterol: 0mg | Sodium: 40mg | Total Carbohydrates: 33g | Dietary Fiber: 5g | Sugar: 3g | Protein: 6g

Instructions:

1. In a medium saucepan, bring the quinoa and almond milk to a boil over medium heat.

2. Reduce the heat to low and simmer for 15 minutes, stirring occasionally, until the quinoa absorbs most of the liquid.

3. Stir in the chia seeds, cinnamon, vanilla extract, and maple syrup (if using). Cook for an additional 2-3 minutes, until the chia seeds begin to thicken the porridge.

4. Remove from heat and let the porridge sit for 5 minutes to fully thicken.

5. Divide the porridge into bowls and top with chopped almonds, fresh berries, and flaxseeds (if using).

Serving Suggestions:

- Serve warm with a drizzle of almond milk for extra creaminess.

Scrambled Eggs with Spinach

- **Preparation Time:** 10 minutes
- **Serves:** 2
- **Size per Serving:** 1 plate (about 150g)

Ingredients:

- 4 large eggs
- 1 cup fresh spinach, chopped
- 1 tablespoon olive oil
- 2 tablespoons unsweetened almond milk
- Salt and pepper to taste

Nutritional Information: Calories: 180 | Total Fat: 14g | Saturated Fat: 3g | Cholesterol: 200 mg | Sodium: 180mg | Total Carbohydrates: 2g | Dietary Fiber: 1g | Sugar: 1g | Protein: 12g

Instructions:

1. Crack the eggs into a bowl and whisk with almond milk, salt, and pepper.

2. Add olive oil to a non-stick pan and warm it over medium heat.

3. Incorporate the chopped spinach and cook until it wilts, which should take about 1-2 minutes.

4. Pour the egg mixture over the spinach and gently scramble with a spatula, stirring constantly until the eggs are fully cooked but still soft, about 3-4 minutes.

5. Remove from heat and serve immediately.

Serving Suggestions:

- Serve with a side of fresh avocado slices or whole grain toast for a balanced, protein-rich breakfast.

Gluten-Free Apple Cinnamon Baked Oatmeal

- **Preparation Time:** 40 minutes
- **Serves:** 6
- **Size per Serving:** 1 square (about 150g)

Ingredients:

- 2 cups gluten-free rolled oats
- 1 teaspoon ground cinnamon
- 1 teaspoon baking powder
- 1/4 teaspoon salt
- 1 1/2 cups unsweetened almond milk
- 1/4 cup unsweetened applesauce
- 1/4 cup pure maple syrup

- 2 large eggs
- 1 teaspoon vanilla extract
- 1 medium apple, peeled and diced

Nutritional Information: Calories: 210 | Total Fat: 4g | Saturated Fat: 0.5g | Cholesterol: 55mg | Sodium: 180mg | Total Carbohydrates: 38g | Dietary Fiber: 5g | Sugar: 12g | Protein: 6g

Instructions:

1. Preheat your oven to 350°F (175°C).
2. In a large bowl, stir together the oats, cinnamon, baking powder, and salt.
3. In a separate bowl, whisk together the almond milk, applesauce, maple syrup, eggs, and vanilla extract until smooth.
4. Combine the wet ingredients with the dry ingredients and stir until mixed, then gently fold in the diced apple.
5. Pour the prepared mixture into an 8x8-inch baking dish that has been greased.
6. Place in the oven and bake for 30-35 minutes, or until the top is nicely browned and the center is firm.
7. Let it cool for 5 minutes before slicing into squares.

Serving Suggestions:

- Serve warm with a dollop of unsweetened yogurt or a drizzle of extra maple syrup.

Buckwheat Almond Waffles

- **Preparation Time:** 20 minutes
- **Serves:** 4
- **Size per Serving:** 1 waffle (about 100g)

Ingredients:

- 1 cup buckwheat flour
- 1/4 cup almond flour
- 1 teaspoon baking powder
- 1/2 teaspoon cinnamon
- 1/4 teaspoon salt
- 1 large egg
- 1 cup unsweetened almond milk
- 1 tablespoon maple syrup (optional)
- 1 teaspoon vanilla extract
- 2 tablespoons coconut oil, melted

Nutritional Information: Calories: 200 | Total Fat: 12g | Saturated Fat: 4g | Cholesterol: 35mg | Sodium: 190 mg | Total Carbohydrates: 20g | Dietary Fiber: 3g | Sugar: 3g | Protein: 6g

Instructions:

1. Preheat your waffle iron and grease lightly with coconut oil.

2. In a large bowl, mix together buckwheat flour, almond flour, baking powder, cinnamon, and salt.

3. In a separate bowl, whisk the egg, almond milk, maple syrup, vanilla extract, and melted coconut oil.

4. Pour the wet mixture into the dry ingredients and stir gently until they are just combined.

5. Pour the batter into the preheated waffle iron and cook according to your waffle maker's instructions, usually about 3-4 minutes or until golden brown.

6. Remove the waffles from the iron and make additional batches with the remaining batter.

Serving Suggestions:

- Top with fresh berries and a dollop of unsweetened Greek yogurt or almond butter for added protein and nutrients.

Lunch Recipes

Grilled Salmon and Kale Salad

- **Preparation Time:** 20 minutes
- **Serves:** 2
- **Size per Serving:** 1 bowl (~250g)

Ingredients:

- 2 (4 oz) salmon filets
- 4 cups kale, chopped
- 1/2 avocado, sliced
- 1/4 cup cherry tomatoes, halved
- 1/4 cup cucumber, sliced
- 1 tbsp olive oil (for massaging kale)
- 1 tbsp olive oil (for grilling)
- 1 tbsp lemon juice
- Salt and pepper to taste
- 1 tbsp hemp seeds or chia seeds (optional for extra omega-3)

Nutritional Information: Calories: 350 | Total Fat: 24g | Saturated Fat: 4g | Cholesterol: 60mg | Sodium: 200mg | Total Carbohydrates: 12g | Dietary Fiber: 7g | Sugar: 2g | Protein: 25g

Instructions:

1. Prepare a grill or grill pan by heating it to medium. Rub the salmon filets with olive oil and season with salt and pepper.

2. Grill the salmon for about 3-4 minutes on each side until cooked through. Set aside to cool slightly.

3. While the salmon is grilling, place the chopped kale in a large bowl. Drizzle 1 tbsp olive oil and lemon juice over the kale, and massage the leaves with your hands until softened (about 2 minutes).

4. Add the cherry tomatoes, cucumber, and avocado slices to the kale.

5. Once the salmon has cooled down a little, crumble it into bite-sized pieces and toss it with the salad.

6. Sprinkle with hemp or chia seeds if using. Toss lightly to combine.

Serving Suggestions:

- Serve immediately as a fresh, nutrient-packed lunch.
- Pair with a light soup or some gluten-free crackers for added texture.

Sardines on Sweet Potato "Toast"

- **Preparation Time:** 20 minutes
- **Serves:** 2
- **Size per Serving:** 1 sweet potato slice with sardines (~150g)

Ingredients:

- 1 medium sweet potato
- 1 (3.75 oz) can sardines in olive oil, drained
- 1/2 avocado, mashed
- 1/2 lemon, juiced
- Salt and pepper to taste
- Fresh dill or parsley for garnish (optional)

Nutritional Information: Calories: 360 | Total Fat: 20g | Saturated Fat: 3g | Cholesterol: 50mg | Sodium: 180mg | Total Carbohydrates: 34g | Dietary Fiber: 6g | Sugar: 6g | Protein: 14g

Instructions:

1. Preheat the oven to 400°F (200°C).
2. Slice the sweet potato into 1/2-inch thick rounds. Arrange them on a baking sheet and lightly coat with olive oil, salt, and pepper.

3. Bake for about 20 minutes or until tender and slightly crispy.

4. In a small bowl, mix the mashed avocado with lemon juice, salt, and pepper.

5. Once the sweet potato rounds are done, spread the avocado mixture on each slice.

6. Top with sardines and garnish with fresh dill or parsley if desired.

Serving Suggestions:

- Enjoy as an open-faced sandwich for lunch.

- These sweet potato toasts can be made ahead and assembled just before serving.

Tuna, Veggie & Quinoa Salad

- **Preparation Time:** 15 minutes

- **Serves:** 2

- **Size per Serving:** 1 bowl (~250g)

Ingredients:

- 1 cup cooked quinoa

- 1 (5 oz) can tuna in water, drained

- 1/2 cup cucumber, diced

- 1/2 cup bell pepper, diced (any color)

- 1/4 cup red onion, finely chopped (optional, adjust based on preference)
- 1/4 cup cherry tomatoes, halved
- 2 tbsp olive oil
- 1 tbsp lemon juice
- Salt and pepper to taste
- Fresh parsley or cilantro for garnish (optional)

Nutritional Information: Calories: 320 | Total Fat: 14g | Saturated Fat: 2g | Cholesterol: 35mg | Sodium: 200mg | Total Carbohydrates: 30g | Dietary Fiber: 5g | Sugar: 2g | Protein: 22g

Instructions:

1. In a large bowl, combine the cooked quinoa, drained tuna, cucumber, bell pepper, red onion, and cherry tomatoes.
2. Combine the olive oil, lemon juice, salt, and pepper in a small bowl, whisking until thoroughly mixed.
3. Add the dressing to the quinoa mixture and stir gently until everything is evenly mixed.
4. Adjust seasoning if needed and garnish with fresh parsley or cilantro if desired.

Serving Suggestions:

- Serve chilled or at room temperature as a nutritious and satisfying lunch.

Turkey and Avocado Collard Green Wraps

- **Preparation Time:** 15 minutes
- **Serves:** 2
- **Size per Serving:** 1 wrap

Ingredients:

- 2 large collard green leaves, stems removed
- 6 oz sliced turkey breast (nitrate-free, low sodium)
- 1/2 ripe avocado, sliced
- 1/4 cup shredded carrots
- 1/4 cup thinly sliced cucumber
- 1 tbsp Dijon mustard
- 1 tbsp hummus (optional for added flavor)
- 1 tsp lemon juice

Nutritional Information: Calories: 280 | Total Fat: 14g | Saturated Fat: 2g | Cholesterol: 50mg | Sodium: 300mg | Total Carbohydrates: 12g | Dietary Fiber: 7g | Sugar: 2g | Protein: 24g

Instructions:

1. Lay the collard green leaves flat and gently spread a thin layer of Dijon mustard on each leaf.
2. Layer the turkey slices evenly on top of the collard leaves.
3. Add avocado slices, shredded carrots, and cucumber on top of the turkey.
4. Drizzle a little lemon juice over the fillings for added flavor.
5. Optionally, spread hummus on the inner side of the leaves for extra taste.
6. Gently roll the collard greens into a wrap, tucking in the sides to secure the filling, then cut the wraps in half for easier handling.

Serving Suggestions:

- Serve with a side of fresh fruit, such as apple slices, or pair with a light salad for a complete, balanced lunch.

Lentil and Tuna Salad in Bell Pepper Boats

- **Preparation Time:** 15 minutes
- **Serves:** 2
- **Size per Serving:** 1 bell pepper boat (~200g)

Ingredients:

- 1 cup cooked lentils (green or brown)
- 1 (5 oz) can tuna in water, drained
- 1 small red onion, finely chopped
- 1 small cucumber, diced
- 1/2 cup cherry tomatoes, halved
- 1 tablespoon olive oil
- 1 tablespoon lemon juice
- Salt and pepper to taste
- 2 large bell peppers, of any color, cut in half and seeded
- Fresh parsley for garnish (optional)

Nutritional Information: Calories: 280 | Total Fat: 9g | Saturated Fat: 1g | Cholesterol: 20mg | Sodium: 250mg | Total Carbohydrates: 30g | Dietary Fiber: 8g | Sugar: 4g | Protein: 20g

Instructions:

1. In a mixing bowl, combine cooked lentils, tuna, red onion, cucumber, and cherry tomatoes.
2. Drizzle with olive oil and lemon juice. Season with salt and pepper. Mix well to combine.
3. Halve the bell peppers, clear out the seeds, and fill each half with the lentil and tuna mix.
4. Garnish with fresh parsley if desired.

Serving Suggestions:

- Serve at room temperature or chilled for a refreshing bite.

Tempeh and Vegetable Stir-fry

- **Preparation Time:** 15 minutes
- **Serves:** 2
- **Size per Serving:** 1 cup (~250g)

Ingredients:

- 1 cup tempeh, cubed
- 1 tablespoon olive oil
- 1 cup bell peppers, sliced (any color)
- 1 cup broccoli florets
- 1 cup snap peas
- 2 cloves garlic, minced

- 1 tablespoon low-sodium soy sauce (or coconut aminos for gluten-free)
- Salt and pepper to taste
- 1 teaspoon sesame seeds (optional)

Nutritional Information: Calories: 300 | Total Fat: 15g | Saturated Fat: 2g | Cholesterol: 0mg | Sodium: 200mg | Total Carbohydrates: 24g | Dietary Fiber: 8g | Sugar: 3g | Protein: 20g

Instructions:

1. Set a large skillet over medium heat and add olive oil to warm it.
2. Add the cubed tempeh and cook for 5-7 minutes, stirring occasionally until lightly browned.
3. Add the bell peppers, broccoli, snap peas, and minced garlic to the skillet. Stir-fry for another 5 minutes until the vegetables are tender-crisp.
4. Drizzle in the low-sodium soy sauce and season with salt and pepper. Stir well to combine.
5. Enjoy hot, with sesame seeds as a garnish if you like.

Serving Suggestions:

- This stir-fry pairs beautifully with brown rice or quinoa for a balanced meal.

Egg Salad Lettuce Cups

- **Preparation Time:** 10 minutes
- **Serves:** 2
- **Size per Serving:** 4 lettuce cups (~150g)

Ingredients:

- 4 hard-boiled eggs, peeled and chopped
- 1 tablespoon plain Greek yogurt (dairy-free if needed)
- 1 tablespoon Dijon mustard
- Salt and pepper to taste
- 1 tablespoon fresh chives, chopped (or green onion)
- 1 tablespoon fresh dill, chopped (optional)
- 4 large lettuce leaves (e.g., romaine or butter lettuce)

Nutritional Information: Calories: 200 | Total Fat: 10g | Saturated Fat: 2g | Cholesterol: 270 mg | Sodium: 210mg | Total Carbohydrates: 6g | Dietary Fiber: 1g | Sugar: 1g | Protein: 20g

Instructions:

1. In a bowl, gently fold together the chopped hard-boiled eggs, Greek yogurt, and Dijon mustard.
2. Season with salt and pepper, then mix in the chives and dill (if using).

3. Lay the lettuce leaves on a plate and scoop the egg salad into each leaf.

4. Serve immediately or refrigerate until it's time to enjoy.

Serving Suggestions:

- They pair well with a side of carrot sticks or sliced cucumbers for added crunch.

Baked Falafel with Tahini Sauce and Cucumber Salad

- **Preparation Time:** 25 minutes
- **Serves:** 4
- **Size per Serving:** 3 falafel balls with 1/4 cup salad (~150g)

Ingredients:

- 1 can of chickpeas (15 oz), thoroughly drained and rinsed
- 1/4 cup fresh parsley, chopped
- 1/4 cup fresh cilantro, chopped
- 1/4 cup onion, finely chopped
- 2 cloves garlic, minced
- 1 teaspoon cumin

- 1 teaspoon coriander
- 1/2 teaspoon baking powder
- 1/4 teaspoon salt
- 1/4 teaspoon black pepper
- 1 tablespoon olive oil (for drizzling)

For the Tahini Sauce:

- 1/4 cup tahini
- 2 tablespoons lemon juice
- 2 tablespoons water
- 1 clove garlic, minced
- Salt to taste

For the Cucumber Salad:

- 1 cup cucumber, diced
- 1 cup cherry tomatoes, halved
- 1 tablespoon olive oil
- 1 tablespoon lemon juice
- Salt and pepper to taste

Nutritional Information: Calories: 220 | Total Fat: 11g | Saturated Fat: 1g | Cholesterol: 0mg | Sodium: 150mg | Total Carbohydrates: 25g | Dietary Fiber: 7g | Sugar: 2g | Protein: 8g

Instructions:

1. Preheat your oven to 375°F (190°C) and use parchment paper to line a baking sheet.

2. In a food processor, combine chickpeas, parsley, cilantro, onion, garlic, cumin, coriander, baking powder, salt, and pepper. Pulse until a coarse mixture forms, being careful not to over-process.

3. Form the mixture into 1-tablespoon-sized balls and set them on the baking sheet. Drizzle with olive oil.

4. Bake for 20-25 minutes, turning halfway through the cooking process, until they are golden and crisp.

5. For the tahini sauce, whisk together tahini, lemon juice, water, garlic, and salt in a small bowl until smooth.

6. For the cucumber salad, combine cucumber, cherry tomatoes, olive oil, lemon juice, salt, and pepper in a bowl and toss well.

7. Serve the falafel warm with tahini sauce and cucumber salad on the side.

Serving Suggestions:

- The falafel can be served in whole grain wraps or over a bed of mixed greens for a nutritious meal.

Cauliflower Rice-Stuffed Bell Peppers

- **Preparation Time:** 30 minutes
- **Serves:** 4
- **Size per Serving:** 1 stuffed bell pepper (~200g)

Ingredients:

- 4 medium bell peppers (any color)
- 1 medium head cauliflower, grated into rice-sized pieces
- 1 cup black beans, drained and rinsed
- 1 cup corn (fresh or frozen)
- 1 teaspoon cumin
- 1 teaspoon paprika
- 1/2 teaspoon garlic powder
- 1/4 teaspoon salt
- 1/4 teaspoon black pepper
- 1 tablespoon olive oil
- 1/4 cup fresh cilantro, chopped (for garnish)

Nutritional Information: Calories: 150 | Total Fat: 5g | Saturated Fat: 1g | Cholesterol: 0mg | Sodium: 180mg | Total Carbohydrates: 22g | Dietary Fiber: 7g | Sugar: 3g | Protein: 6g

Instructions:

1. Preheat the oven to 375°F (190°C).
2. Cut off the tops of the bell peppers, remove the seeds, and set them upright in a baking dish.
3. Set a large skillet over medium heat and add olive oil to warm it. Add grated cauliflower and sauté for 5-7 minutes until slightly softened.
4. Stir in black beans, corn, cumin, paprika, garlic powder, salt, and pepper. Cook for an additional 2-3 minutes, mixing well.
5. Stuff each bell pepper with the cauliflower mixture, pressing down gently to pack it in.
6. Cover the baking dish with aluminum foil and bake for 25 to 30 minutes, or until the peppers become tender.
7. Garnish with fresh cilantro before serving.

Serving Suggestions:

- Serve these stuffed peppers with a side salad or sliced avocado for a complete meal.
- They can also be topped with a dollop of plain yogurt for added creaminess.

Grilled Chicken and Vegetable Salad

- **Preparation Time:** 25 minutes
- **Serves:** 4
- **Size per Serving:** 1 bowl (~250g)

Ingredients:

- 2 boneless chicken breasts, skinless, weighing around 1 pound.
- 2 tablespoons olive oil
- 1 teaspoon Italian seasoning
- Salt and pepper to taste
- 4 cups of mixed salad greens, including spinach, arugula, and romaine.
- 1 cup cherry tomatoes, halved
- 1 medium cucumber, sliced
- 1 bell pepper, sliced
- 1/4 cup balsamic vinegar

Nutritional Information: Calories: 220 | Total Fat: 10g | Saturated Fat: 1g | Cholesterol: 70mg | Sodium: 150mg | Total Carbohydrates: 10g | Dietary Fiber: 3g | Sugar: 3g | Protein: 28g

Instructions:

1. Get the grill or grill pan ready by preheating it over medium-high heat.

2. Drizzle olive oil over the chicken breasts and sprinkle with Italian seasoning, salt, and pepper.

3. Grill chicken for 6-7 minutes on each side, or until fully cooked (internal temperature should reach 165°F/74°C).

4. Once removed from the grill, let the chicken rest for a few minutes before cutting into it.

5. Toss the salad greens, cherry tomatoes, cucumber, and bell pepper together in a large bowl.

6. Drizzle the salad with balsamic vinegar and toss gently to combine.

7. Top the salad with sliced grilled chicken.

Serving Suggestions:

- This salad pairs well with whole grain crackers or a side of hummus for added nutrients.

Dinner Recipes

Grilled Shrimp with Asparagus

- **Preparation Time:** 20 minutes
- **Serves:** 4
- **Size per Serving:** 1 cup

Ingredients:

- 1 pound (450g) large shrimp, peeled and deveined
- 1 bunch asparagus, trimmed
- 2 tablespoons olive oil
- 2 cloves garlic, minced
- 1 teaspoon lemon juice
- 1 teaspoon paprika
- Salt and pepper to taste
- Fresh lemon wedges (for serving)

Nutritional Information: Calories: 250 | Total Fat: 10g | Saturated Fat: 1g | Cholesterol: 150mg | Sodium: 200mg | Total Carbohydrates: 10g | Dietary Fiber: 3g | Sugar: 2g | Protein: 30g

Instructions:

1. Preheat the grill to medium-high heat.

2. In a bowl, combine shrimp, asparagus, olive oil, garlic, lemon juice, paprika, salt, and pepper. Toss until well-coated.

3. Thread shrimp onto skewers and place asparagus alongside them on the grill.

4. Grill for 3-4 minutes on each side, or until the shrimp are pink and opaque, and the asparagus is tender.

5. Remove from the grill and serve immediately with fresh lemon wedges.

Serving Suggestions:

- Pair with a side salad of mixed greens and cherry tomatoes for added nutrients.

Baked Halibut with Roasted Brussels Sprouts

- **Preparation Time:** 10 minutes (plus 20 minutes cooking time)
- **Serves:** 4
- **Size per Serving:** 1 filet of halibut with 1 cup of Brussels sprouts

Ingredients:

- 4 halibut filets (about 6 oz each)

- 2 tablespoons olive oil
- 1 lemon, juiced
- 2 garlic cloves, minced
- Salt and pepper to taste
- 1 pound Brussels sprouts, trimmed and halved
- 1 teaspoon dried thyme

Nutritional Information: Calories: 280 | Total Fat: 15g | Saturated Fat: 2g | Cholesterol: 70mg | Sodium: 150mg | Total Carbohydrates: 12g | Dietary Fiber: 4g | Sugar: 2g | Protein: 28g

Instructions:

1. Preheat the oven to 400°F (200°C).
2. In a bowl, mix olive oil, lemon juice, minced garlic, salt, and pepper.
3. Place the halibut filets on a baking sheet lined with parchment paper and brush both sides with the marinade.
4. In another bowl, toss the halved Brussels sprouts with olive oil, thyme, salt, and pepper.
5. Spread them on the same baking sheet around the halibut.

6. Bake for 20 minutes or until the halibut flakes easily with a fork and the Brussels sprouts are tender and slightly crispy.

7. Serve immediately.

Serving Suggestions:

- Pair with a side of quinoa or brown rice for added fiber and nutrients.

Herb-Crusted Chicken Breast with Steamed Broccoli

- **Preparation Time:** 10 minutes (plus 25 minutes cooking time)
- **Serves:** 4
- **Size per Serving:** 1 chicken breast with 1 cup of broccoli

Ingredients:

- 4 boneless, skinless chicken breasts
- 2 tablespoons olive oil
- 1 teaspoon garlic powder
- 1 teaspoon onion powder
- 1 teaspoon dried oregano
- 1 teaspoon dried thyme

- Salt and pepper to taste
- 4 cups broccoli florets

Nutritional Information: Calories: 230 | Total Fat: 10g | Saturated Fat: 1.5g | Cholesterol: 75mg | Sodium: 200mg | Total Carbohydrates: 6g | Dietary Fiber: 2g | Sugar: 2g | Protein: 32g

Instructions:

1. Preheat the oven to 375°F (190°C).
2. In a small bowl, mix olive oil, garlic powder, onion powder, oregano, thyme, salt, and pepper to create a marinade.
3. Place chicken breasts in a baking dish and brush both sides with the marinade.
4. Bake in the preheated oven for 25 minutes or until the chicken is cooked through and reaches an internal temperature of 165°F (75°C).
5. As the chicken bakes, steam the broccoli florets until they are soft, which should take about 5-7 minutes.
6. Serve the chicken with steamed broccoli on the side.

Serving Suggestions:

- Garnish with lemon wedges for a fresh flavor and serve with quinoa or brown rice for a complete meal.

Turkey and Vegetable Zucchini Noodle Lasagna

- **Preparation Time:** 45 minutes
- **Serves:** 6
- **Size per Serving:** 1 slice

Ingredients:

- 2 medium zucchinis, spiralized into noodles
- 1 pound ground turkey (lean)
- 1 cup spinach, chopped
- 1 cup mushrooms, diced
- 1 cup low-sodium marinara sauce
- 1 cup ricotta cheese (part-skim)
- 1 cup shredded part-skim mozzarella cheese
- 1 tablespoon olive oil
- 1 teaspoon dried basil
- 1 teaspoon garlic powder
- Salt and pepper to taste

Nutritional Information: Calories: 290 | Total Fat: 14g | Saturated Fat: 6g | Cholesterol: 75mg | Sodium: 350mg | Total Carbohydrates: 10g | Dietary Fiber: 3g | Sugar: 5g | Protein: 30g

Instructions:

1. Preheat the oven to 375°F (190°C).

2. Using a skillet, heat olive oil to medium heat. Add the ground turkey and cook until browned, seasoning it with salt, pepper, garlic powder, and basil.

3. Add spinach and mushrooms to the skillet, cooking until the vegetables are tender. Remove from heat.

4. In a baking dish, layer half of the zucchini noodles on the bottom. Spread half of the ricotta cheese over the noodles, followed by half of the turkey mixture and half of the marinara sauce. Repeat the layers, finishing with a layer of marinara sauce on top.

5. Sprinkle mozzarella cheese over the top layer.

6. Place aluminum foil over the dish and bake for 25 minutes.

7. Give it a few minutes to cool down before you cut it into slices.

Serving Suggestions:

- Serve warm, paired with a side salad or steamed vegetables to make it a complete meal.

Baked Eggplant Rounds with Tomato Sauce

- **Preparation Time:** 30 minutes
- **Serves:** 4
- **Size per Serving:** 2 eggplant rounds

Ingredients:

- 1 large eggplant, sliced into ½-inch rounds
- 1 cup homemade or low-sodium tomato sauce
- 1 cup shredded part-skim mozzarella cheese
- 1 tablespoon olive oil
- 1 teaspoon dried oregano
- 1 teaspoon garlic powder
- Salt and pepper to taste
- Fresh basil leaves for garnish (optional)

Nutritional Information: Calories: 180 | Total Fat: 9g | Saturated Fat: 3g | Cholesterol: 15mg | Sodium: 300mg | Total Carbohydrates: 18g | Dietary Fiber: 6g | Sugar: 4g | Protein: 10g

Instructions:

1. Preheat the oven to 400°F (200°C).

2. Arrange eggplant rounds on a baking sheet lined with parchment paper. Brush both sides with olive oil and season with salt, pepper, oregano, and garlic powder.

3. Place in the oven for 15 minutes, turning halfway through, until the eggplant is tender and slightly browned.

4. Remove from the oven and spoon tomato sauce over each round. Sprinkle mozzarella cheese on top.

5. Place back in the oven and continue baking for 10 minutes, or until the cheese is melted and bubbling.

6. Garnish with fresh basil before serving.

Serving Suggestions:

- Serve warm alongside a salad of mixed greens and a light vinaigrette.

Baked Cod with Tomato and Olive Tapenade

- **Preparation Time:** 30 minutes
- **Serves:** 4
- **Size per Serving:** 1 filet

Ingredients:

- 4 cod filets (about 6 ounces each)

- 1 cup cherry tomatoes, halved
- 1/2 cup black olives, pitted and chopped
- 2 tablespoons capers, rinsed and drained
- 2 tablespoons olive oil
- 1 teaspoon dried oregano
- 1 lemon, juiced
- Salt and pepper to taste
- Fresh parsley, chopped (for garnish)

Nutritional Information: Calories: 230 | Total Fat: 10g | Saturated Fat: 1g | Cholesterol: 70mg | Sodium: 360mg | Total Carbohydrates: 7g | Dietary Fiber: 2g | Sugar: 2g | Protein: 30g

Instructions:

1. Preheat the oven to 400°F (200°C).

2. In a bowl, mix the cherry tomatoes, black olives, capers, olive oil, oregano, lemon juice, salt, and pepper.

3. Place the cod filets on a baking sheet lined with parchment paper. Spoon the tomato and olive mixture evenly over each filet.

4. Place the cod in the preheated oven and bake for 15 to 20 minutes, or until it turns opaque and flakes easily with a fork.

5. Once it's out of the oven, garnish with freshly chopped parsley before serving.

Serving Suggestions:

- Serve with quinoa or brown rice and a side of steamed green beans or broccoli for a balanced meal.

Mushroom and Pea Risotto

- **Preparation Time:** 10 minutes (plus 30 minutes cooking time)
- **Serves:** 4
- **Size per Serving:** 1 cup

Ingredients:

- 1 cup Arborio rice
- 4 cups low-sodium vegetable broth
- 1 cup mushrooms, sliced (e.g., cremini or button)
- 1 cup frozen peas
- 1 small onion, finely chopped
- 2 garlic cloves, minced
- 2 tablespoons olive oil
- 1/4 cup nutritional yeast (for a cheesy flavor)

- Salt and pepper to taste
- Fresh parsley, chopped (for garnish)

Nutritional Information: Calories: 250 | Total Fat: 8g | Saturated Fat: 1g | Cholesterol: 0mg | Sodium: 150mg | Total Carbohydrates: 38g | Dietary Fiber: 4g | Sugar: 2g | Protein: 8g

Instructions:

1. In a saucepan, slowly heat the vegetable broth over low heat to keep it at a warm temperature.
2. Set a large skillet over medium heat and add olive oil to warm it. Toss in the chopped onion and garlic, and sauté until they are soft and translucent.
3. Add sliced mushrooms and cook until they release moisture and become tender.
4. Add the Arborio rice, cooking for 1-2 minutes until the rice is just slightly toasted.
5. Gradually add the warm vegetable broth in one ladle at a time, stirring often, and wait until the liquid is largely absorbed before adding more.
6. After about 15 minutes, add the frozen peas. Continue adding broth until the rice is creamy and al dente, about 25-30 minutes total.

7. Mix in the nutritional yeast, salt, and pepper to taste, then remove from heat and garnish with fresh parsley before serving.

8. Remove from heat and finish with a garnish of fresh parsley before serving.

Serving Suggestions:
- Enjoy with steamed vegetables or a crisp green salad for a full dining experience.

Slow-Cooker Lean Beef and Root Vegetable Stew

- **Preparation Time:** 15 minutes (plus 6-8 hours cooking time)
- **Serves:** 6
- **Size per Serving:** 1 bowl

Ingredients:
- 1.5 pounds lean beef stew meat, cut into 1-inch cubes
- 4 medium carrots, sliced
- 3 medium potatoes, diced
- 2 stalks celery, chopped
- 1 medium onion, chopped
- 4 cups low-sodium beef broth

- 2 cloves garlic, minced
- 1 teaspoon dried thyme
- 1 teaspoon dried rosemary
- Salt and pepper to taste
- 1 tablespoon olive oil (for browning, optional)

Nutritional Information: Calories: 290 | Total Fat: 8g | Saturated Fat: 3g | Cholesterol: 70mg | Sodium: 400mg | Total Carbohydrates: 25g | Dietary Fiber: 4g | Sugar: 3g | Protein: 30g

Instructions:

1. In a skillet, heat olive oil over medium-high heat (optional). Add the beef cubes and sear on all sides for approximately 5-7 minutes. (Skip this step if you prefer a simpler method.)
2. Transfer the browned beef to a slow cooker. Add the carrots, potatoes, celery, onion, garlic, thyme, rosemary, salt, and pepper.
3. Pour the beef broth over the ingredients in the slow cooker.
4. Cover and cook on low for 6-8 hours or on high for 3-4 hours, until the beef and vegetables are tender.
5. Stir well before serving.

Serving Suggestions:

- Serve hot, garnished with fresh herbs if desired, and enjoy with whole grain bread for a complete meal.

Stuffed Zucchini Boats

- **Preparation Time:** 15 minutes (plus 30 minutes cooking time)
- **Serves:** 4
- **Size per Serving:** 2 zucchini halves

Ingredients:

- 4 medium zucchinis
- 1 cup cooked quinoa
- 1 cup diced tomatoes (fresh or canned)
- 1 cup black beans, drained and rinsed
- 1 small onion, chopped
- 2 cloves garlic, minced
- 1 teaspoon cumin
- 1 teaspoon paprika
- 1 tablespoon olive oil
- Salt and pepper to taste
- Fresh cilantro, chopped (for garnish)

Nutritional Information: Calories: 220 | Total Fat: 6g | Saturated Fat: 1g | Cholesterol: 0mg | Sodium: 200mg | Total

Carbohydrates: 38g | Dietary Fiber: 10g | Sugar: 4g | Protein: 10g

Instructions:

1. Preheat the oven to 375°F (190°C).
2. Cut the zucchinis in half lengthwise and scoop out the centers using a spoon to create boats. Reserve the pulp.
3. Using a skillet, heat olive oil to medium heat. Add the chopped onion and garlic, and sauté until they reach a soft texture.
4. Stir in the reserved zucchini pulp, diced tomatoes, black beans, cooked quinoa, cumin, paprika, salt, and pepper. Allow it to cook for around 5 minutes, until it's heated all the way through.
5. Spoon the mixture into the zucchini boats, filling them generously.
6. Place the stuffed zucchinis on a baking sheet and bake for 25-30 minutes until the zucchinis are tender.
7. Once removed from the oven, sprinkle fresh cilantro on top before serving.

Serving Suggestions:

- Serve with a side of mixed greens or a simple vinaigrette for a refreshing contrast.

Baked Salmon with Roasted Sweet Potatoes and Green Beans

- **Preparation Time:** 15 minutes (plus 25 minutes cooking time)
- **Serves:** 4
- **Size per Serving:** 1 filet, 1 cup sweet potatoes, 1 cup green beans

Ingredients:

- 4 salmon filets (about 4 ounces each)
- 2 medium sweet potatoes, peeled and cubed
- 2 cups green beans, trimmed
- 2 tablespoons olive oil
- 1 teaspoon garlic powder
- 1 teaspoon paprika
- Salt and pepper to taste
- Fresh lemon wedges (for serving)

Nutritional Information: Calories: 350 | Total Fat: 14g | Saturated Fat: 2g | Cholesterol: 70mg | Sodium: 150mg |

Total Carbohydrates: 35g | Dietary Fiber: 6g | Sugar: 5g | Protein: 25g

Instructions:

1. Preheat the oven to 400°F (200°C).

2. In a large bowl, toss the cubed sweet potatoes with 1 tablespoon of olive oil, garlic powder, paprika, salt, and pepper. Spread them out evenly in a single layer on the baking sheet.

3. Place the sweet potatoes in the preheated oven and bake for 15 minutes.

4. While the sweet potatoes are baking, toss the green beans with the remaining olive oil, salt, and pepper in a separate bowl.

5. After the sweet potatoes have baked for 15 minutes, add the green beans to the baking sheet and place the salmon filets on top. Add a pinch of salt and pepper to the salmon for flavor.

6. Return the baking sheet to the oven and bake for an additional 10-15 minutes, or until the salmon is cooked through and flakes easily with a fork, and the vegetables are tender.

7. Serve immediately, alongside lemon wedges.

Serving Suggestions:

- Pair with a side of quinoa or brown rice for an extra boost of complex carbohydrates.

Desserts and Snacks

Cacao Nut Clusters

- **Preparation Time:** 15 minutes
- **Serves:** 12
- **Size per Serving:** 1 cluster

Ingredients:

- 1 cup mixed nuts (almonds, walnuts, pecans)
- 1/2 cup unsweetened shredded coconut
- 1/4 cup raw cacao powder
- 1/4 cup honey or maple syrup
- 1/4 teaspoon vanilla extract
- Pinch of sea salt

Nutritional Information: Calories: 100 | Total Fat: 8g | Saturated Fat: 2g | Cholesterol: 0mg | Sodium: 10mg | Total Carbohydrates: 10g | Dietary Fiber: 2g | Sugar: 4g | Protein: 3g

Instructions:

1. Preheat your oven to 350°F (175°C).

2. In a large bowl, combine mixed nuts, shredded coconut, raw cacao powder, honey or maple syrup, vanilla extract, and sea salt. Stir until the mixture is smooth and the ingredients are well combined.

3. Scoop tablespoon-sized amounts of the mixture and form into small clusters on a lined baking sheet.

4. Bake in the preheated oven for about 10 minutes, or until slightly golden.

5. Remove from the oven and cool completely on the baking sheet, allowing the clusters to harden.

Serving Suggestions:

- Serve as a snack or dessert.

- These clusters pair well with a glass of almond milk or can be enjoyed with fresh fruit for added nutrition.

Strawberry Coconut Oat Bars

- **Preparation Time:** 20 minutes
- **Serves:** 12
- **Size per Serving:** 1 bar

Ingredients:

- 2 cups rolled oats
- 1 cup unsweetened shredded coconut
- 1/2 cup almond butter or peanut butter

- 1/2 cup honey or maple syrup
- 1 cup fresh strawberries, chopped
- 1 teaspoon vanilla extract
- Pinch of salt

Nutritional Information: Calories: 150 | Total Fat: 7g | Saturated Fat: 3g | Cholesterol: 0mg | Sodium: 50mg | Total Carbohydrates: 22g | Dietary Fiber: 3g | Sugar: 8g | Protein: 4g

Instructions:

1. Preheat your oven to 350°F (175°C) and prepare an 8x8-inch baking dish by lining it with parchment.

2. In a large bowl, mix together the rolled oats, shredded coconut, almond butter, honey or maple syrup, chopped strawberries, vanilla extract, and salt until well combined.

3. Pour the mixture into the prepared baking dish and press it down firmly with a spatula or your hands to create an even layer.

4. Bake in the preheated oven for 25-30 minutes, or until the edges are a nice golden hue.

5. Allow the bars to cool completely in the pan before lifting them out and cutting into squares.

Serving Suggestions:

- Keep these bars fresh by storing them in an airtight container in the refrigerator for a week.

Dried Fruit Energy Nuggets

- **Preparation Time:** 15 minutes
- **Serves:** 12
- **Size per Serving:** 1 nugget

Ingredients:

- 1 cup mixed dried fruits (such as apricots, dates, and raisins)
- 1 cup raw nuts (such as almonds or walnuts)
- 1/2 cup unsweetened nut butter (such as almond or cashew butter)
- 1/4 cup honey or maple syrup
- 1 teaspoon cinnamon
- Pinch of salt

Nutritional Information: Calories: 80 | Total Fat: 5g | Saturated Fat: 1g | Cholesterol: 0mg | Sodium: 5mg | Total Carbohydrates: 10g | Dietary Fiber: 2g | Sugar: 6g | Protein: 2g

Instructions:

1. Combine the mixed dried fruits and raw nuts in a food processor and pulse until they are finely chopped, but not pureed.

2. Add the nut butter, honey or maple syrup, cinnamon, and salt to the processor. Blend until the mixture holds together.

3. Scoop out small amounts of the mixture and roll them into balls or nugget shapes using your hands.

4. Place the nuggets on a parchment-lined tray and refrigerate for at least 30 minutes to firm up.

Serving Suggestions:

- These energy nuggets make a great snack.

Baked Cinnamon Pears with Walnuts

- **Preparation Time:** 10 minutes
- **Serves:** 4
- **Size per Serving:** 1 pear half

Ingredients:

- 2 ripe pears, halved and cored
- 1/2 cup chopped walnuts
- 2 tablespoons honey or maple syrup
- 1 teaspoon cinnamon

- 1/2 teaspoon vanilla extract
- Pinch of salt

Nutritional Information: Calories: 150 | Total Fat: 7g | Saturated Fat: 1g | Cholesterol: 0mg | Sodium: 10mg | Total Carbohydrates: 20g | Dietary Fiber: 3g | Sugar: 10g | Protein: 3g

Instructions:

1. Preheat your oven to 350°F (175°C).
2. Place the pear halves cut side up in a baking dish.
3. In a small bowl, combine chopped walnuts, honey or maple syrup, cinnamon, vanilla extract, and salt. Mix well.
4. Spoon the walnut mixture evenly over the pear halves.
5. Bake in the preheated oven for 20-25 minutes, until the pears are tender and the walnuts are lightly toasted.

Serving Suggestions:

- Serve warm as a healthy dessert or snack.
- Pair with a dollop of plain yogurt or a scoop of nut butter for added creaminess.

Mixed Berry Salad with Mint and Lemon

- **Preparation Time:** 15 minutes
- **Serves:** 4
- **Size per Serving:** 1 cup

Ingredients:

- 1 cup strawberries, hulled and sliced
- 1 cup blueberries
- 1 cup raspberries
- 1 cup blackberries
- 2 tablespoons fresh mint leaves, chopped
- 1 tablespoon honey (optional)
- Juice of 1 lemon
- Zest of 1 lemon

Nutritional Information: Calories: 80 | Total Fat: 0.5g | Saturated Fat: 0g | Cholesterol: 0mg | Sodium: 5mg | Total Carbohydrates: 20g | Dietary Fiber: 5g | Sugar: 12g | Protein: 1g

Instructions:

1. In a large bowl, combine the strawberries, blueberries, raspberries, and blackberries.

2. In a small bowl, whisk together honey (if using), lemon juice, and lemon zest until well combined.

3. Drizzle the dressing over the mixed berries and add the chopped mint. Toss gently to combine.

4. Serve at once, or refrigerate for 30 minutes to allow the flavors to meld.

Serving Suggestions:

- Enjoy as a refreshing snack or dessert.

Smoothies

Almond Butter Banana Smoothie

- **Preparation Time:** 5 minutes
- **Serves:** 2
- **Size per Serving:** 1 cup (250 ml)

Ingredients:

- 2 ripe bananas, sliced
- 2 tablespoons almond butter (unsweetened)
- 1 cup of unsweetened almond milk (or any other non-dairy milk you like)
- 1 tablespoon chia seeds (optional)
- 1 teaspoon vanilla extract
- Ice cubes (optional)

Nutritional Information: Calories: 210 | Total Fat: 9g | Saturated Fat: 1g | Cholesterol: 0mg | Sodium: 105mg | Total Carbohydrates: 30g | Dietary Fiber: 4g | Sugar: 12g | Protein: 6g

Instructions:

1. In a blender, combine the sliced bananas, almond butter, almond milk, chia seeds, and vanilla extract.
2. If you want a colder smoothie, toss in some ice cubes.
3. Blend until smooth and creamy.
4. Taste and adjust sweetness by adding more bananas if desired.
5. Pour into glasses and enjoy immediately.

Serving Suggestions:

- Top with a sprinkle of chia seeds or a few banana slices for added texture and nutrition.

Berry and Spinach Smoothie

- **Preparation Time:** 5 minutes
- **Serves:** 2
- **Size per Serving:** 1 cup (250 ml)

Ingredients:

- 1 cup of mixed berries (fresh or frozen options like strawberries, blueberries, and raspberries)

- 1 cup fresh spinach leaves
- 1 medium banana, peeled
- 1 cup of unsweetened almond milk (or any other non-dairy milk you like)
- 1 tablespoon chia seeds (optional)
- Ice cubes (optional)

Nutritional Information: Calories: 120 | Total Fat: 2g | Saturated Fat: 0g | Cholesterol: 0mg | Sodium: 40mg | Total Carbohydrates: 25g | Dietary Fiber: 5g | Sugar: 12g | Protein: 3g

Instructions:

1. In a blender, combine the mixed berries, spinach, banana, and almond milk.
2. If using, add chia seeds for added fiber and omega-3 fatty acids.
3. Toss in some ice cubes for a cooler consistency, if you prefer.
4. Blend until smooth and creamy.
5. Taste and adjust sweetness if needed (you can add a little honey or maple syrup if desired).
6. Pour into glasses and serve immediately.

Serving Suggestions:

- Top with a few whole berries or a sprinkle of chia seeds for added texture.

Cucumber and Green Apple Smoothie

- **Preparation Time:** 10 minutes
- **Serves:** 2
- **Size per Serving:** 1 cup (250 ml)

Ingredients:

- 1 medium cucumber, peeled and chopped
- 1 green apple, cored and chopped
- 1 cup fresh spinach leaves
- Juice of 1 lemon
- 1 cup unsweetened coconut water
- 1 tablespoon fresh ginger, grated (optional)
- Ice cubes (optional)

Nutritional Information: Calories: 70 | Total Fat: 0g | Saturated Fat: 0g | Cholesterol: 0mg | Sodium: 5mg | Total Carbohydrates: 17g | Dietary Fiber: 3g | Sugar: 10g | Protein: 1g

Instructions:

1. In a blender, combine the chopped cucumber, green apple, spinach leaves, lemon juice, and coconut water.
2. Add grated ginger and ice cubes if desired.
3. Blend until smooth and well combined.
4. Taste and, if you prefer a tangier flavor, add more lemon juice as necessary.
5. Pour into glasses and serve immediately.

Serving Suggestions:

- Garnish with cucumber slices or apple wedges.

Mango-Turmeric Smoothie

- **Preparation Time:** 10 minutes
- **Serves:** 2
- **Size per Serving:** 1 cup (250 ml)

Ingredients:

- 1 ripe mango, peeled and diced
- 1 cup fresh spinach leaves
- 1 banana, sliced
- 1 teaspoon ground turmeric
- 1 cup unsweetened almond milk (or any other preferred non-dairy milk)

- 1 tablespoon chia seeds (optional)

- Ice cubes (optional)

Nutritional Information: Calories: 150 | Total Fat: 4g | Saturated Fat: 0g | Cholesterol: 0mg | Sodium: 40mg | Total Carbohydrates: 30g | Dietary Fiber: 5g | Sugar: 18g | Protein: 3g

Instructions:

1. In a blender, combine the diced mango, spinach leaves, banana, turmeric, and almond milk.

2. Add chia seeds and ice cubes if desired.

3. Blend until smooth and creamy.

4. Taste and adjust sweetness or thickness by adding more almond milk if necessary.

5. Pour into glasses and serve immediately.

Serving Suggestions:

- Serve with a sprinkle of extra turmeric or chia seeds on top.

Carrot, Ginger, and Orange Smoothie

- **Preparation Time:** 5 minutes
- **Serves:** 2
- **Size per Serving:** 1 cup (250 ml)

Ingredients:

- 1 cup carrots, peeled and chopped
- 1 medium orange, peeled and segmented
- 1 teaspoon fresh ginger, grated
- 1 cup of unsweetened almond milk (or any other non-dairy milk you like)
- 1 tablespoon maple syrup (optional)
- Ice cubes (optional)

Nutritional Information: Calories: 110 | Total Fat: 1g | Saturated Fat: 0g | Cholesterol: 0mg | Sodium: 30mg | Total Carbohydrates: 26g | Dietary Fiber: 4g | Sugar: 12g | Protein: 2g

Instructions:

1. In a blender, combine the chopped carrots, orange segments, grated ginger, and almond milk.
2. If desired, add maple syrup for extra sweetness.
3. If you want a colder smoothie, toss in some ice cubes.
4. Blend until smooth and well combined.

5. Taste and adjust sweetness if necessary.

6. Pour into glasses and serve immediately.

Serving Suggestions:

- Garnish with a sprinkle of grated ginger or a slice of orange on the rim of the glass.

CHAPTER 3

30 Days Meal Plan

Please note that the provided meal plan is a sample and should not be interpreted as a recommendation to consume all the listed recipes in a single day.

This meal plan aims to offer inspiration and guidance for healthy meal preparation. Feel free to customize this plan to suit your preferences and dietary requirements.

Day 1

- **Breakfast:** Sweet Potato and Black Bean Breakfast Bowl
- **Lunch:** Turkey and Avocado Collard Green Wraps
- **Dinner:** Grilled Shrimp with Asparagus
- **Dessert/Snack:** Cacao Nut Clusters
- **Smoothie:** Mango-Turmeric Smoothie

Day 2

- **Breakfast:** Blueberry Oat Pancakes
- **Lunch:** Grilled Salmon and Kale Salad
- **Dinner:** Baked Eggplant Rounds with Tomato Sauce
- **Dessert/Snack:** Strawberry Coconut Oat Bars
- **Smoothie:** Cucumber and Green Apple Smoothie

Day 3

- **Breakfast:** Quinoa and Chia Seed Breakfast Porridge
- **Lunch:** Tuna, Veggie & Quinoa Salad
- **Dinner:** Turkey and Vegetable Zucchini Noodle Lasagna
- **Dessert/Snack:** Dried Fruit Energy Nuggets
- **Smoothie:** Almond Butter Banana Smoothie

Day 4

- **Breakfast:** Smashed Peas and Avocado Toast
- **Lunch:** Sardines on Sweet Potato "Toast"
- **Dinner:** Baked Cod with Tomato and Olive Tapenade
- **Dessert/Snack:** Baked Cinnamon Pears with Walnuts
- **Smoothie:** Carrot, Ginger, and Orange Smoothie

Day 5

- **Breakfast:** Turkey and Spinach Egg Muffins
- **Lunch:** Lentil and Tuna Salad in Bell Pepper Boats
- **Dinner:** Slow-Cooker Lean Beef and Root Vegetable Stew
- **Dessert/Snack:** Mixed Berry Salad with Mint and Lemon
- **Smoothie:** Berry and Spinach Smoothie

Day 6

- **Breakfast:** Coconut Yogurt Parfait
- **Lunch:** Egg Salad Lettuce Cups
- **Dinner:** Herb-Crusted Chicken Breast with Steamed Broccoli
- **Dessert/Snack:** Cacao Nut Clusters
- **Smoothie:** Mango-Turmeric Smoothie

Day 7

- **Breakfast:** Kale and Mushroom Frittata
- **Lunch:** Tempeh and Vegetable Stir-fry
- **Dinner:** Baked Halibut with Roasted Brussels Sprouts
- **Dessert/Snack:** Strawberry Coconut Oat Bars
- **Smoothie:** Cucumber and Green Apple Smoothie

Day 8

- **Breakfast:** Gluten-Free Apple Cinnamon Baked Oatmeal
- **Lunch:** Cauliflower Rice-Stuffed Bell Peppers
- **Dinner:** Mushroom and Pea Risotto
- **Dessert/Snack:** Dried Fruit Energy Nuggets
- **Smoothie:** Almond Butter Banana Smoothie

Day 9

- **Breakfast:** Scrambled Eggs with Spinach
- **Lunch:** Grilled Chicken and Vegetable Salad

- **Dinner:** Stuffed Zucchini Boats
- **Dessert/Snack:** Baked Cinnamon Pears with Walnuts
- **Smoothie:** Carrot, Ginger, and Orange Smoothie

Day 10

- **Breakfast:** Buckwheat Almond Waffles
- **Lunch:** Turkey and Avocado Collard Green Wraps
- **Dinner:** Baked Salmon with Roasted Sweet Potatoes and Green Beans
- **Dessert/Snack:** Mixed Berry Salad with Mint and Lemon
- **Smoothie:** Berry and Spinach Smoothie

Day 11

- **Breakfast:** Sweet Potato and Black Bean Breakfast Bowl
- **Lunch:** Grilled Salmon and Kale Salad
- **Dinner:** Baked Eggplant Rounds with Tomato Sauce
- **Dessert/Snack:** Cacao Nut Clusters
- **Smoothie:** Mango-Turmeric Smoothie

Day 12

- **Breakfast:** Blueberry Oat Pancakes
- **Lunch:** Tuna, Veggie & Quinoa Salad

- **Dinner:** Turkey and Vegetable Zucchini Noodle Lasagna
- **Dessert/Snack:** Strawberry Coconut Oat Bars
- **Smoothie:** Cucumber and Green Apple Smoothie

Day 13

- **Breakfast:** Quinoa and Chia Seed Breakfast Porridge
- **Lunch:** Sardines on Sweet Potato "Toast"
- **Dinner:** Baked Cod with Tomato and Olive Tapenade
- **Dessert/Snack:** Dried Fruit Energy Nuggets
- **Smoothie:** Almond Butter Banana Smoothie

Day 14

- **Breakfast:** Smashed Peas and Avocado Toast
- **Lunch:** Lentil and Tuna Salad in Bell Pepper Boats
- **Dinner:** Slow-Cooker Lean Beef and Root Vegetable Stew
- **Dessert/Snack:** Baked Cinnamon Pears with Walnuts
- **Smoothie:** Carrot, Ginger, and Orange Smoothie

Day 15

- **Breakfast:** Turkey and Spinach Egg Muffins
- **Lunch:** Egg Salad Lettuce Cups

- **Dinner:** Herb-Crusted Chicken Breast with Steamed Broccoli
- **Dessert/Snack:** Mixed Berry Salad with Mint and Lemon
- **Smoothie:** Berry and Spinach Smoothie

Day 16
- **Breakfast:** Coconut Yogurt Parfait
- **Lunch:** Tempeh and Vegetable Stir-fry
- **Dinner:** Baked Halibut with Roasted Brussels Sprouts
- **Dessert/Snack:** Cacao Nut Clusters
- **Smoothie:** Mango-Turmeric Smoothie

Day 17
- **Breakfast:** Kale and Mushroom Frittata
- **Lunch:** Grilled Chicken and Vegetable Salad
- **Dinner:** Mushroom and Pea Risotto
- **Dessert/Snack:** Strawberry Coconut Oat Bars
- **Smoothie:** Cucumber and Green Apple Smoothie

Day 18
- **Breakfast:** Gluten-Free Apple Cinnamon Baked Oatmeal
- **Lunch:** Cauliflower Rice-Stuffed Bell Peppers
- **Dinner:** Stuffed Zucchini Boats
- **Dessert/Snack:** Dried Fruit Energy Nuggets

- **Smoothie:** Almond Butter Banana Smoothie

Day 19

- **Breakfast:** Scrambled Eggs with Spinach
- **Lunch:** Turkey and Avocado Collard Green Wraps
- **Dinner:** Baked Salmon with Roasted Sweet Potatoes and Green Beans
- **Dessert/Snack:** Baked Cinnamon Pears with Walnuts
- **Smoothie:** Carrot, Ginger, and Orange Smoothie

Day 20

- **Breakfast:** Buckwheat Almond Waffles
- **Lunch:** Grilled Salmon and Kale Salad
- **Dinner:** Grilled Shrimp with Asparagus
- **Dessert/Snack:** Mixed Berry Salad with Mint and Lemon
- **Smoothie:** Berry and Spinach Smoothie

Day 21

- **Breakfast:** Sweet Potato and Black Bean Breakfast Bowl
- **Lunch:** Tuna, Veggie & Quinoa Salad
- **Dinner:** Turkey and Vegetable Zucchini Noodle Lasagna
- **Dessert/Snack:** Cacao Nut Clusters
- **Smoothie:** Mango-Turmeric Smoothie

Day 22

- **Breakfast:** Blueberry Oat Pancakes
- **Lunch:** Sardines on Sweet Potato "Toast"
- **Dinner:** Baked Cod with Tomato and Olive Tapenade
- **Dessert/Snack:** Strawberry Coconut Oat Bars
- **Smoothie:** Cucumber and Green Apple Smoothie

Day 23

- **Breakfast:** Quinoa and Chia Seed Breakfast Porridge
- **Lunch:** Lentil and Tuna Salad in Bell Pepper Boats
- **Dinner:** Slow-Cooker Lean Beef and Root Vegetable Stew
- **Dessert/Snack:** Dried Fruit Energy Nuggets
- **Smoothie:** Almond Butter Banana Smoothie

Day 24

- **Breakfast:** Smashed Peas and Avocado Toast
- **Lunch:** Egg Salad Lettuce Cups
- **Dinner:** Herb-Crusted Chicken Breast with Steamed Broccoli
- **Dessert/Snack:** Baked Cinnamon Pears with Walnuts
- **Smoothie:** Carrot, Ginger, and Orange Smoothie

Day 25

- **Breakfast:** Turkey and Spinach Egg Muffins
- **Lunch:** Tempeh and Vegetable Stir-fry
- **Dinner:** Baked Halibut with Roasted Brussels Sprouts
- **Dessert/Snack:** Mixed Berry Salad with Mint and Lemon
- **Smoothie:** Berry and Spinach Smoothie

Day 26

- **Breakfast:** Coconut Yogurt Parfait
- **Lunch:** Grilled Chicken and Vegetable Salad
- **Dinner:** Mushroom and Pea Risotto
- **Dessert/Snack:** Cacao Nut Clusters
- **Smoothie:** Mango-Turmeric Smoothie

Day 27

- **Breakfast:** Kale and Mushroom Frittata
- **Lunch:** Cauliflower Rice-Stuffed Bell Peppers
- **Dinner:** Stuffed Zucchini Boats
- **Dessert/Snack:** Strawberry Coconut Oat Bars
- **Smoothie:** Cucumber and Green Apple Smoothie

Day 28

- **Breakfast:** Gluten Free Apple Cinnamon Baked Oatmeal
- **Lunch:** Lentil and Tuna Salad in Bell Pepper Boats

- **Dinner:** Stuffed Zucchini Boats
- **Dessert/Snack:** Dried Fruit Energy Nuggets
- **Smoothie:** Almond Butter Banana Smoothie

Day 29

- **Breakfast:** Scrambled Eggs with Spinach
- **Lunch:** Egg Salad Lettuce Cups
- **Dinner:** Baked Halibut with Roasted Brussels Sprouts
- **Dessert/Snack:** Baked Cinnamon Pears with Walnuts
- **Smoothie:** Carrot, Ginger, and Orange Smoothie

Day 30

- **Breakfast:** Buckwheat Almond Waffles
- **Lunch:** Grilled Chicken and Vegetable Salad
- **Dinner:** Turkey and Vegetable Zucchini Noodle Lasagna
- **Dessert/Snack:** Mixed Berry Salad with Mint and Lemon
- **Smoothie:** Berry and Spinach Smoothie

CHAPTER 4

Conclusion

As you close this cookbook, remember that you're not just holding a collection of recipes—you're grasping a powerful tool for nurturing your child's health and well-being.

Throughout these pages, you've discovered how the right foods can support your child's brain function, potentially easing ADHD symptoms and boosting overall wellness.

You've learned that feeding a child with ADHD isn't about restriction, but about abundance—an abundance of nutrient-rich, whole foods that fuel the body and mind.

From colorful breakfast bowls to satisfying dinners, you now have a repertoire of delicious meals that your whole family can enjoy together.

Remember, every meal you prepare is an act of love and support for your child. You're not just filling their stomachs; you're nourishing their potential, one bite at a time.

The journey may have its challenges, but you're equipped with knowledge and a variety of tasty options to keep your child engaged and excited about healthy eating.

As you implement these recipes into your daily life, be patient and observant. Notice how different foods affect your child's mood, focus, and energy levels.

Use this awareness to further customize their diet, always keeping in mind that each child is unique. Remember that diet is just a single piece in the bigger health picture.

Combine these nutritious meals with regular exercise, adequate sleep, and supportive therapies as recommended by your healthcare provider. Together, these elements create a strong foundation for your child's success.

Finally, celebrate your efforts and the positive changes you're making. You're doing something incredible for your child, setting them up for a lifetime of healthier choices.

Trust in the process, stay consistent, and know that with every wholesome meal you serve, you're helping your child thrive. Here's to your family's health and happiness—bon appétit!

Made in the USA
Monee, IL
27 April 2025

16452582R00057